W0259444

POWER

BALLADS

GARRETT CAPLES

POWER BALLADS

WAVE BOOKS

SEATTLE AND NEW YORK

Published by Wave Books. www.wavepoetry.com. Copyright © 2016 by Garrett Caples. All rights reserved Wave Books titles are distributed to the trade by Consortium Book Sales and Distribution. Phone: 800-283-3572 / SAN 631-760X. Library of Congress Cataloging-in-Publication Data. Names: Caples, Garrett T., author. Title: Power ballads / Garrett Caples. Description: Seattle : Wave Books, [2016]. Identifiers: LCCN 2015044537 | ISBN 9781940696379 (limited edition hardcover) | ISBN 9781940696362 (softcover). Classification: LCC PS3603.A662 A6 2016 | DDC 811/.6—dc23. LC record available at http://lccn.loc.gov/2015044537. Designed by Quemadura. Printed in the United States of America. 9 8 7 6 5 4 3 2 1. First Edition. Wave Books 059.
Some of these poems appeared in *AMERARCANA*, *Aufgabe*, *Big Bell*, *Brooklyn Rail*, *Ladowich*, *OmniVerse*, *A Sharp Piece of Awesome*, *TC.HE*, *Try*, *Volt*, and *Where Eagles Dare*, and in the chapbooks *Invisible Sleep* (Auguste Press, 2013) and *What Surrealism Means to Me* (Gas Meter, 2014). *Gut of Brando* (Free Poetry, 2011) was issued as a pamphlet by Martin Corless-Smith and also appeared on the City Lights Blog (blogcitylights.com). "Nod Often" appeared on CAConrad's *Philly Sound* (phillysound.blogspot.com) in 2009. "Love Is Made of Sky" was written for a Jeff Mellin EP of that title (dPulse Recordings, 2010) featuring Doug Yule on bass and the first line is taken from "I'm a Lover," off the album *Poet Song* (Vanguard Records, 1969) by Tina and David Meltzer. A subliminal point is the juxtaposition of their band Serpent Power ("Endless Tunnel," etc.) with Velvet Underground ("Venus in Furs," etc.). John Ashbery used a line from this poem as the epigraph for "Warm Regards" from *Breezeway* (Ecco, 2015)—right on! "The Chosen" contains two fragments from "When Doves Cry" from *Purple Rain* (Warner Bros., 1984) by Prince and the Revolution. "Chiefly" contains two lines from "Revolutionary Letter #11" from *Revolutionary Letters* (City Lights, 1971) by Diane di Prima and two lines from "I Don't Give a Fuck" from *2pacalypse Now* (Interscope, 1991) by 2Pac. "Richard O. Moore Imagined as a Bob Dylan Song" contains a line from "Shelter from the Storm" and a line from "If You See Her, Say Hello" from *Blood on the Tracks* (Columbia, 1975) by Bob Dylan, while "Tractatus" is named after *Tractatus Logico-Philosophicus* (Kegan Paul, 1922) by Richard's favorite philosopher, and mine, Wittgenstein. "Dark Candle" contains a phrase, "crystal forehead," from a Fulke Greville poem but I can't remember which. It's dedicated to my shrink. "Garrett Caples Rides Again" has a fragment from a John Ashbery poem but I can't remember which (from either *A Wave* [1984] or *Houseboat Days* [1977]). There's also a line from Slade's non-album single "Thanks for the Memory" (Polydor, 1975) and a line from a Wallace Stevens poem, "Earthy Anecdote," in *Harmonium* (Knopf, 1923). "Self-Portrait as David Letterman" was originally published as "The Garrett Caples Show." "Paul Bowles in El Cerrito" begins with a sentence from *The Delicate Prey and Other Stories* (Random House, 1950) by Paul Bowles. "Self-Portrait as James Bond" contains a line from every James Bond theme through *Skyfall* (MGM, 2012) and was written for the Bond-themed compilation album *A Girl and a Gun* (wiaiwya, 2015). (Did it ever actually happen?) "Zen of Nez" contains fragments of "Grand Ennui" from *Nevada Fighter* (RCA, 1971) by Michael Nesmith and the First National Band and the title song of *Diamond Dogs* (RCA, 1974) by David Bowie. "Ten Ten-Line Poems for Philip Lamantia" has a line from "Man Is in Pain" from *Ekstasis* (Auerhahn, 1959) by Philip Lamantia. "Celtic Love Song for Suzanne" derives from Taliesin as translated in *The Celts* (Inner Traditions, 1993) by Jean Markale. I found a copy in a (since-relocated) used bookstore (Forest) in the Mission in San Francisco, en route to an early date with Suzanne. *avid diva* was published in 2010 as an installment of the Lew Gallery series edited by Sunnylyn Thibodeaux and Micah Ballard; the title came from a tangled lanyard I saw on the subway. I wrote "Road Song for Juan and the Pines" for that group's lead singer and rhythm guitarist, Julian Talamantez Brolaski. "The Chosen," "Feel My Pain," and "Hypnagogic Boston" appeared in the 2012 video *Three Poems* (dir. Brian Lucas and DJ Impereal) on thevolta.org; shout out to Marco, Bruce, Nani, Niche (RIP). "Hypnagogic Boston" contains a phrase, "Mrs. God," from Keith Richards's *Life* (Little, Brown & Co., 2010). The *Power Ballads* concept emerged from a discussion with Jackson Meazle at The Liberties in San Francisco.

THIS BOOK IS FOR SUZANNE

Stayin' up for days in the Chelsea Hotel
Writin' "Sad-Eyed Lady of the Lowlands" for you

BOB DYLAN, "Sara," *Desire* (1976)

POWER BALLADS

POWER BALLADS

AVID DIVA

avid diva, visit me
dispense divine advice
o radiant deviant

evidence of violence
rivets my vivid dive
addictive desire violates me

drives my rivers
in reverse, revives
my velvet revolution

revs my vacuum cleaner
that died, veils my veins
with unbelievable sleeves

divides evening into
eternities laced with
invisible sleep

my valves go viral
my values on vacation
my vultures counterclockwise

they prey on my vices
the liver rippers! the wind
invents voices on the wing

to whisper livid
prayers above my
vibrating window

listen, avid diva
i have a hive nearby
i invite you to

a hovel i've chosen
close to the oval of love
run up my vacant stairs

invade my ventilation
shaft and fill my vats
with quivering liquid

video my elvis selves
in silver levis swiveling
vote in my next erection

save me, avid diva
in advance of the broken
arm, advocate for the victim

who avoids your eyes
to envision the void
devour his heart

provoke my vital signs
i survived just in time
for your give it to me

leaving me heaving in
tears of repulsive beauty
i'm not vegas or jesus

i'm recovering
belief in the everyday
rave against time

days i want to live, days
i want to die, days i'm
the luckiest man alive

HYPNAGOGIC BOSTON

by the little screen
where I lie with the dogs
and live with no drugs
and ponder the ponderosa
beneath this heat where
my flaming feet repeat
the steps I missed
the first last time around
a lossless ratio stations itself
on guard against the density
of imperfected memories
I send postcards abroad
to mister & missus god
asking if clarity begins at home
and hope the answer's no
I know the script's too cryptic
to decipher aboard this floating horse
tell the doctor when to expect
my corpse to arrive by riverboat
slowly befitting my dignity

PAUL SCHEERBART

FOR ANDREW JORON

i wandered the impossible
in search of perpetual motion
the protagonist of my novel
was glass architecture
i went broke from agonistic loves
i mourn the books i never wrote:
a handbook of the foot
an insider's guide to bullshit
my *technical treatise on paper plates*
would've run 4000 pages
but only sold one copy
(because i'd lose my author copy)
what i wrote about didn't exist
but you couldn't make me up
my mustache waxed and waned
gravy stains buttoned my coat
long after food became memory
sadly i was mistaken on
the dirigible's endurance
but i pretty much called skyscrapers
and aerial bombardment
here i am in the past a futurist

a steam punk with dry heaves
in a guttapercha gutter
in my last glass act
i wrote my assassin's name
on fogged up pince nez
and flung them away
with transparent childlike grace

they evicted the man behind my beard
he tickled

LOVE IS MADE OF SKY

love is a movie we watch ourselves in, a film we wash ourselves in. a sky that looks askance at the lack of scandalousness in even the most licentious thought. the song of the beleaguered dispatcher herding taxis together, or the hiss of inflatable ramps sliding down desire. love is a cloud in the sky that's also love. i remember today like it was yesterday. i open a door and there stands love, ready to get down, and i'm like whoa, we just met and love's like i don't care. love has a history of such indiscretions. a baby wailing on an electric fivestring banjo during a piano recital in the library of a redeye flight to boston could no more disconcert than love when love comes to town on a fine arab charger or even a budweiser clydesdale. love drives whatever it wants and frankly prefers something furrier than the average fuzzy dice. the velvet cheesesteak applepie of the snowbound vermont mind is dismissed by love as missing the point of the needle, its flawless tenderness and penchant for cool appraising stares below the roof of its woolhat horizon. love instead noodles nile delta blues at 79 rpms. the rpgs of love explode at the antipodes of saint dope island and carnal canal, for love wreaks magic havoc with the music of public life. love loves it when love does it because love is a moonlit boxingglove giving the finger to violence. a sky we look upon that tumbles and falls, and a bright blue sun in the sky. love is a risky sky.

THE CHOSEN

FOR DAVID MELTZER

when two of us meet
we know one another
by insight, by the brio
we rock the quicksilver
with or the weird succor
we offer ourselves in a
mirror of single minds

the way our fingers
twitch around improvised
amulets, the signet burnt
on our sunburst guitars

or the altitude inside
our supine attitude

a ghost of uncertain
courtesy sets aside
its scythe to admire
the view, animals strike
curious poses, posers
see and taste and hate

they feel the heat of
two of us meeting

when two of us meet
we've known ourselves
all along, an infinite
unforgetting of the time
another two of us met

we are only part of us

the rest is an ego ago
adrift in a silent age
we burn the candle
straight down the middle

a moment is a table
we pull up chairs to
to look with naked eye
upon eternity

THE HYDROPATHIC WAY

FOR CEDAR & MICAH

I need another song today, something to sing to the boys at the bar to thank them for being there. The more I fold the petals of the brass rose called my life the more I sense their drunk abundance in five-minute phonecalls and handsome ransom notes. When I'm hammered on the anvil underfoot, they reintroduce that discontinued line of goods long enough to stock my shelves for a spell. I pull up in a coffin but skate away on silver blades, to the cathedral of our next encounter, already being built. I try to leave the hard stuff back at the mausoleum but their whiskey holds the key to the city, whistling nonchalantly. Maybe just this once again I'll bend to the tawny brim, but only in august company. If I were an eleventh-century Japanese prince, I'd write it on pearl-white paper and fix sprigs of fir to the envelope, and send it off and retire dignified to the garden, and I'd look to the sky and the cold would sting my wide-open eyes. Instead I'm iMacking at 1:00 a.m., eyes slit like turrets, taking a shot at the poem with the ammo of memory. Like the song says, they're in my hair and that's a good look for me.

CHIEFLY

here i am king of this ghost republic
in love's conspicuous absence

flatfooted & redhanded
in stuttering abandon

i enter her charming apartments
in search of evidence: how to live

among altars to the dead & alive
it's chiefly a mental space whose

lucid clutter produces utter clarity
now & then. against the bent

of the amplified hick party
she posts letters to the present

like *he's got nothing in common*
with the men who run his mind

it takes a certain kind of nerve
to learn to persevere like this

mama told me there'd be days like this
but i'm pissed 'cause it stays like this

to pray for bliss & face abyss
puts a dent in the teeth. thankfully

my beak can still wreak havoc
on my self-esteem as equally

& comfort eludes me
carrot & stick

AFTER DIANE DI PRIMA & 2PAC

ROAD SONG FOR JUAN & THE PINES

brian's in thailand
andy's in the azores
cedar's in new york

i'm in the mission
with micah & patrick
writing poems with titles

like *living the kindle*
maia's in chinatown
erin's chicagobound

johnny cash is dead
but ain't no grave
can hold him down

lorca's just born
in fillmore, cybele's
stuck in tucson &

fuck if i know how
david's in piedmont
city of millionaires

marco's off to medellín
when he finds someone
to look after his dogs

rob bought a house
in the laurel district
by *glenn's hot dogs*

up 35th from east 14th
where dontrell lives
in his studio. tonight

greg's in berkeley
rupert's in east anglia
teaching philosophy &

richard's in mill valley
writing it. i got a jeff in
philly, a jeff in ypsilanti

& a geoff with a g
in bakersfield with
a pedal steel guitar

& SHE still lives
two blocks away
& tears me up inside

RICHARD O. MOORE IMAGINED AS A BOB DYLAN SONG

as a child back in ohio
they gambled for my toys
they loaded up a pickup truck
with my relatives & tore
off for another part of america
leaving me behind
in a county home in L.A.
for the orphaned & the blind

i learned to be invisible
a naked camera eye
a lamppost by a lighthouse
an antenna in your side
i wasn't made for handgrenades
i was made for making signs
i heard the noise behind each word
the notes in every sigh

i met railroad poets, potentates
rock royalty, potential mates
posers & composers & fate
decreed i orchestrate

experience through templates
executives could tolerate
if it came in underbudget
& within the bounds of taste

they kicked me offa campus
& i quit a couple jobs
i made penicillin for the willing
shooting movies for the mobs
still my poems followed me
like undomesticated dogs
the world was all that was the case
in my arguments with god

at first devoid of virtue
& lastly cleansed of pride
i flouted death's selection
by accidentally surviving
but she still lives inside of me
a creature without form
on the pages of my yesterdays
i'll keep tomorrow warm

LOST POEM

FOR CEDAR

the typewriter at work yields its ink for this one
automatic poem, and i'll chuck in some leaves and
pineapples and other colorful stuff, to give to the man
with the one big bowl. this poem is done in oriental rugs
and oriental drugs, such as the kind makers used to mother.
its opposable thumb is hitching a ride across the bay
because the subway is full of smoke. i've been listening
to keith richards all day and reading philip lamantia and
just generally sitting around with the battery idle, waiting
for that almost midnight freedom. he's out there partying now
and i'm almost there with him, if i can find the cross-street.
being a poet in san francisco is much like this, even though
i live in oakland.

HOMAGE TO ROD ROLAND

ah man, an inch of snow in cairo
& peter o'toole dies same day
as joan fontaine. pete's death
hurts the rest of us who were
n't affected by, say, paul walker
's child molestation explosion
but still gotta live with it in the
cosmic sense. i cried when john
ny thunders died & laughed a
bout kurt cobain though maybe
that's just me. my-my-my gener
ation didn't include me for reasons
not opaque to me. i wasn't what
mtv said to be & it was a comp
elling narrative back then. i listen
to the filler on an iron butterfly
album & think why'd they bother
when they just coulda? i hear ele
phants are telepathic & why
shouldn't they be? they got
big ears

DARK CANDLE

FOR MARIA PILAR BRATKO

my crystal forehead
lacks a backbone
o dark candle
illumine me

my lamp is damp
with doggy dew
waterlogged shoes
squish beneath my feet

laughter in my slaughter
house drowns out
touch of mothertough
thought

i talk through a tank
of my own design
a glass bowl full
of smoke

i draw hash marks
on a calendar hung
in a horrid corridor
to idontknowwhat

destination. i walk
backwards through time
like those african guys
who say the future

comes from behind
because we can't see
the future. they know
how it goes down

my past gives me
the evil eye even as
its highbeams ride
my bumper

delight it, dark candle
refuse its engine
& change its regime
another game emerges

from the margins
of my bargain
basement
unconscious

teeth. i can't split
my lips without a lisp
like a venom viper
in a denim diaper

my poison slips
through coiled icicles
i beg your dark apartment
to thaw the thwarted

art of myself

FEEL MY PAIN

i drill into the noun
beneath the verb
to find an ugly

word. i'm having
my own fucking
hostage crisis

& what kinda way
to break the ice is
that? the third hand

of god—damn!
flips me off & on
& often i've gone

nuts just because
. like a character
in someone else's

novel i've lost
narrative control:
how embarrassing

i have to feel &
feel i have. i
cry like a fire

& run like a sore
i highfive a spider
in a hemorrhoid rage

feel my pain &
please explain why
suffering's made me

a total pussy.

MY BLACK DIARY

is dedicated to someone i hate. begins with an invocation, called *l'envoi* in the renaissance, an address to the reader separate from the main text. the shade *coca-cola red* is borrowed from messy marv. it turns into an allusion to *alice in wonderland*, the tenniel drawings of frog footmen. remedios varo paintings crossed with at least one section written after watching *buffalo '66*. a response to a poem secretly alluding to me, the last verse a line from *sea-eclogues* by william diaper. a column of bitterness and silence around the time of 9/11, one-word lines like robert lax though not intentionally and nothing like him really. a post–9/11 attack on the way poets talked about politics, then a reckoning of a time when the legends who still walked the earth began to disappear into death: realignment of the cosmos. there follows an old hollywood anecdote almost exactly as told to me. a surrealist meditation on american history incorporating a phrase from my then-psychiatrist. a pot poem inspired by a restaurant experience with andrew joron, incorporating notes from an edition of edward young's *night thoughts* and alluding to the contents of a late-1800s *oakland tribune*. it continues with a song inspired by a chinese painting and tales of the ghost house in san francisco. a barthesian fantasia on america's resistance to the dollar coin. a collage of the most frequently used nouns in *touch of the marvelous*. three poems for someone i used to know. impressions of beijing and xi'an. what i wrote on 9/11. an essay on ambrose bierce. an expression limited to the number of double-o words i could find. four sets of liner notes, one unused. a parody of the memoir craze. a congressional address. an elegy for a musician including a line from renoir's *the river*. an elegy for an apartment. an elegy for a poet. an elegy for a relative. an elegy for my best friend. an elegy for myself. it ends in 306 one-word lines composed entirely in four-letter words. its bright covers might mislead you.

GARRETT CAPLES RIDES AGAIN

my concealed carry personality
has deformed my trouser content

to the extent my permit permits
i'm shooting off often in public

i'm a blow dart in a wind tunnel
aimed in the wrong direction

a boycotted russian vodka distiller
an assdial away from arrest

i'm that bad molly going around
on the business end of fucking up

that's me in the glass inner office
telling beads on the heads of my foes

is it genderqueer to be a femme
& such an aggressive asshole

same bat time, same bat channel
but the cosplay's a satin hassle

you'd think my years in a boyband
would inure me to humiliation

but this bratwurst from the king
is the only thing keeping me

was i going to say alive? was i
going to stay in & get things done

or stand in line for a cronut
at my age in this tax bracket

they said bananas could get you high
they said lyric poems had to die

they said lickon tattoos were lsd
& toiletseats could give you stds

the reek of the schoolyard cistern
haunts today's items of piety

just as readily but to me the poetry
only grows under such conditions

as to hold the candle up to the album
to illuminate the grooves. every time

the bucks go clattering i go numbering
their hooves in this inexplicable ritual

of anthropologizing up over this
200 year old carpet of cigarettes

i'm ready for my autotune, dr. luke
i'm ready to head to toluca lake

to watch the ghosts of flappers
float over the lawn of the hope estate

while it's still for sale. where once
i was cuckoo for cocoapuffs

i'm afraid i've gone apeshit
for grapenuts today. i've only got

so many colons to lasso
your heart away

BLAP

the frauds that give the art a bad name
the flautists and flauntists and haunted cornballs
the hardened badgers, bargers, and barterers
the candystripers with maximum backpack
the stalls in the horserace engineblock that got the art nowhere
the gold i left in your care that you chose to invest in a losing hand
or buried in sand and forgot where you left the map
the occasional fuck do i have to do everything feeling
that overcomes me like yeah, the game needs me
that siren song the city of oakland emits
the weird realization that i, odysseus, am home
here or else crashed out on that reef
that i'm at home enough i might finally leave
for the love of another human being
the helium you see me breathe easily
or the cartesian delirium you'd hardly believe
takes place along trespasses of passover lanes
the games you don't want to play or be good sports at
at the scatman crothers hong kong phooey memorial suite
or the willie the lion smith dreyfusard cannonball run
or the desmond tutu nine-millimeter bible toss
the things you don't know shit about
that could fill a clickthru agreement
or a henry ford chick-fil-a achievement
vanessa time, vanessa place, vanessa motion
vanessa grease, vanessa way, vanessa feeling

OAKLAND

i love my city

huey newton
first declared
oakland occupied
in a very different
sense

more like paris
or baghdad

forty years later
& suddenly

THE TOWN
dogged the flame
from zuccotti park

new yorkers chanted
we are oakland
& even in egypt
they knew

i love my city

the priced out
progressives of
san francisco
entered the
panther cage

explosive combo
to rock the dome
of robocop

our summer of love
was an autumn of blood
in the neolexicon

but i love my city
cuz we mean
peace

demonstrated
repeatedly
at the 2011
general strike:

nonviolence
='d no police

& so many poets
there & boots
from the coup

& later i'm told
rexroth & lamantia
were at the last
general strike
in '46 & i'm like

i love my city

birthplace of scrapers
& scraper bikes

home at one time
to gertrude stein
earl fatha hines
alden van buskirk
erich von stroheim

too short & 2pac
shock-g & sheila e
baby jaymes
larry graham &
pharoah sanders

i'll take j.stalin
over jay z any day

occupy all streets?
occupy deez

i love my city

in massachusetts
lawrence &
andover

in new jersey
piscataway &
new brunswick

in brighton
england

in berkeley
california

i hated living

not until oakland
did i love home

i've lived here
fifteen years

it's been a long
long reckoning
since i first laid
eyes on leaving
but now it's
at hand

i could be like
fuck it, it's gone
duck dynasty
on me but i'd
be kidding me

i miss it like
a horny lover
& i haven't
yet left

o oakland
black city
i've known
your ghettos

stone city to
murder dubs

the lower bottoms
the ’corns &
cypress

ghosttown
dogtown
jingletown

call me danny
from sobrante
keak da sneak
or deev da
muthafuckin
greed

there’s no south o
that’s just the bay
sprouting from
heinhold’s first
& last chance

& fuck jack
london & jack
london square

i drink there for
ambrose bierce

the north's called
ice city but also
temescal

which means
sweat house
in nahuatl

& my friend ceels
of *sun poem for ceels*
translates nahuatl

& my friend fab
of *super sic wid it*
put north o on
the rap map

i'm connected here

i saw oscar grant
become an icon
tho i'm sure
he'd rather
be alive

lake merritt poem:
to judge the change
in seasons by

observing water
fowl: red ducks
blue ducks
pelicans &
cranes

the goddamn
geese never leave
the herons hide
in the trees

by the postoffice
where rumor (&
the *new york times*)
had them tossed
in the woodchipper

just like the feds
to pass the buck
to the hapless
subcontractor

they say oakland's
the new brooklyn
but part of it
used to be
brooklyn

know your history
o makers of anthologies

parvenus of telegraph
avenue, i been
been here

on mamas
on see-through
it's lightweight mine

NOD OFTEN

i will sleep
with you

señor
citizen

one drop
in a human
ocean

tear in the
purple earth

pulse beating
itself to death

trying to graft
onto a life

the cyclops
ringing his
bell again

votes himself
worst nightmare

for the third
straight year
in a row

i hesitate
to run him
over

though i
know i
oughta

why me
lord

johnny cash
would ask

who weakened
my weekend

my overdose
overdoes it

needless
needles

courtesy
your local

police state
department
store

plant evidence
grow case

how do you
say stop
looking
at me

to a vacuum
power power
vacuum

sucking off
aloft a loft
the obvious
lobbyist

the genetically
sodomized
botanist

the codified
nine to five
legitimized
colonist

bipartisan
shit agreed
to a greed
long ago

coming soon
a water economy

in an event
known as the
wrinkle disaster

the secretary of
the office of
preoccupied
hiccups

cops a mug
to chug in
the tub &

is found
drowned
afterward

in a note
in another
hand he
laments

even tv
no longer
pretends

to give
a shit
about
you

MARGIN OF TERROR

i'm not your mailman but i know where you live. market research has made you immortal. i'm a fog on your house of mirrors, a drag on your merry-go-round. a safecracker. a safe cracker. a man with his tongue in your ears. a spider who enters your internet. a government. an earwig drawn to your underwear drawer. your transvestite gettysburg ip address. a pistol palace with raunchy guards. america's varicose veins, the bloodclot in its brain. the grey tits of dawn over your appleless orchard. a keychain bible piercing your lips. your oilslick emphasis. the ozone layer you don't remember. a snot rag constitution. your carpet tarpit. the severed black tail of miss waldron's red colobus served on a rainforest 2 × 4. your hysterical stenographer. the controlled demolition of your world trade center. a taser brushing your reefer teeth. queef of baghdad, queef of england, your always identical menu. the gagging goggles of your internal gestapo. death is your only insurance. i've sharpened my knives. i'm not your doctor but i'll take your life.

AMERICA THE POEM

hold your horses and cut the crap: the almighty dollhouse has spoken! welcome to the all-white meet-and-greet, a nuclear overreaction to our plastic propaganda. i read on tv we live in the world's most fortunate cookie, a complex apartment in an apartment complex. the ceiling is leaking but rain'll be worth money someday. the barcode is down the hall to your right; please swipe yourself before you leave. these implants are killing me, but if it keeps me safe! there goes that old alligator with the banana in his ear, off to type up his report. the intersection has eyes if you don't. don't pass out in your passport photo or you'll be blurry in real life and you'll never catch a plane. my baggage claims everything's heavier now. i can barely flip open my phone and the sound quality's like scraping my eardrum with razorwire. i'm ready to retire at thirty-five; time's wasted me so i can't waste time.

TRIUMPH OF THE WILLING

third world war against us, capital US us, so us in the US against the US in us are fucked. enter an agent of chaos in the muddle of good versus legal. with bees flying out my cheeks and ebony anemone eyes. a bag of nostrils over my shoulder, a bone in my cigarette holder. an army of bipolar bears. ohmigod it's avant-garde. a non-lethal spasm disorders your organs at the hands of an armored tux-edo. a gasmask orgasms, headlocks a dreadlock, distorts a reporter, threatens a veteran of foreign wars. hold it, kid hitler, i got a grenade for you. i parade through the gutter dipped in butter to drip on his uniform corn. i hurl camouflage samsonite luggage at the propellers of finance, just to be an asshole. i'll fix me a human casserole in the ultimate world bank parody. don't thank me, i'm just a role model, bathing in lunatic fringe. i cringe on the ledge of my credit card while pitiful capitalists duel with the lower caste. it's hard to be a saint but i enjoy the work; anarchy's more than it's cracked up to be. i keep squares outside my inner circle and only roll with my apostles. i ain't a mess, i'm a messianic pessimist, up against you against us in the US against the US in us. i could drop a cop with a rock in a sock, or pop a glock at a stockbroker's heart, or clock the president with a shoe, but the agent of chaos is useless against you.

PARABLE

One day, when my friend and I were already way past drunk, we began to raid his father's cellar, throwing back whole bottles, leaving others uncorked, untasted, forgotten. In true drunkard's fashion we drank backwards, each vintage augmenting our boldness, leading us to vintages rarer still. We were soused!

Suddenly he ran to the corner to vomit. I had no problem vomiting where I stood.

"Look!" he said.

"No!" I said.

"No—these cases!" He vomited again like a paintball gun.

"These are the last bottles of Fauvieux! My father just bought them at auction." He belched irrelevantly.

I popped the cork on a 100-year-old balthazar of Veuve Clicquot to rinse the vomit from my mouth, but the warm champagne squirted out my nose when I tried to drink from the bottle. I flung it aside in disgust.

"Fauvieux?" I said.

“Yes!” he said. “Fauvieux. It’s this microscopic province in France. At the eastern tip of Burgundy. They’ve been making wine there for hundreds of years.” He stumbled over for a closer look.

There was a stack of five wooden crates, and sure enough *Fauvieux* was stamped in black on the side of each. A crowbar conveniently lay atop the crates, like the steward was interrupted in the task of unpacking them and hadn’t returned to it. My friend began prying open the topmost crate with the crowbar. I went to a recessed corner housing cobwebbed bottles of ancient port and urinated.

When I returned he was holding two hay-specked bottles in the air in triumph.

“Behold! The last of the Fauvieux!” He handed me a bottle and thrust the other between his legs, attacking it with a corkscrew. I looked at the label, a parchment-colored square with the word *Fauvieux* printed in black-letter font over a hand-stamped image of a red salamander, under which the year *1988* was printed.

There was an expectant pause as he fiddled with the cork; I felt I owed him the question.

“So what the fuck happened?”

“In Fauvieux?” he asked, feigning disinterest even as his face brightened like the sun. He loved to tell stories.

He handed me the opened bottle of Fauvieux—which I very nearly dropped—and took the other from me, repeating his fumbling with the corkscrew.

"It's nuts," he said as he split the cork. He pushed the rest of the cork into the bottle with his finger. Real cork!

"It's nuts," he repeated. "You know how France generates most of its energy from nuclear power?"

"No."

"Well, they do. Anyway, they keep their reactors in the east, near the Swiss and German borders."

"The dicks!"

"Yeah," he laughed. "Fuck the French. Anyhow, they had one at the edge of Fauvieux. Well, back in . . ." he consulted the label weavingly ". . . 1988, a pipe leaked a bunch of radioactive shit into the ground—no one knows how long before they found it. Uranium.

"No, wait—it's '89. This stuff is '88. Anyway, this uranium leaked into the groundwater, got in the wells, the river, all the water. So the reactor company dudes and the government dudes go around in their biosuits, telling everyone not to use the water, don't drink it, don't bathe in it, don't water anything. It went on for two weeks, after which they were like, OK, it's safe. And all these herbs they grew there—gone. Nothing that year.

"There's only like five tiny-ass vineyards in Fauvieux—same families for hundreds of years. Or maybe Pernod bought one, but the rest were authentic. Tiny-ass place—you could only get Fauvieux in France, there wasn't enough to export. Rare as fuck, expensive as hell, its own grapes that only grew there, all that shit.

"Anyhow, the vines for some reason still looked cool, so they make the wine, age it and shit. Meanwhile they're trying to grow new grapes, but they're totally fucked. Withered like little raisins. The shit's so fucked they can't make wine out of it. Same thing next year. And the herbs taste like shit of course.

"But they're aging the wine and it seems like it's going cool. But when it's supposed to be ready, like really ready, they try it out, and it sucks! Totally sucks." He paused to vomit, barely breaking stride now that he'd warmed to his tale.

"Destroyed the economy, of course; nothing down there not related to winemaking.

"Anyway, there's been none on the market for years until this estate sale; some old French fuck who had five cases died and dad just had to have them. It was mentioned in the *New York Times*."

I vomited.

"Probably some other douchebags have some stashed away, but this is basically it right here," he said, waving the bottle at me. "The last of the Fauvieux!" He raised his bottle and took a swig.

I took a swig and spit it out to rinse the vomit from my mouth. Then I stepped back as far as I could, about twenty paces, and set the bottle on the floor. I raised my machine gun—we'd been hunting—and began spraying the crates with bullets.

"Holy fuck!" he said. His bottle of Fauvieux shattered on the floor as he dove behind a cask of amontillado. Splinters flew everywhere, chips of stones from the wall, shards of glass from nearby bottles. I emptied the whole clip into the crates and the wine flowed through the bulletholes like blood.

When I finished, I picked up my bottle of Fauvieux, took a swig, and smashed the bottle on the ground. I don't remember how it tasted.

My friend emerged from the cask and stared at the lake of Fauvieux as it gradually soaked into the cellar floor. He turned to me with a pained expression.

"But that was the last of the Fauvieux!"

GUT OF BRANDO

Like another actor affixed to his waist, the gut of Brando plays its part, performs its role, in contradistinction to the gut's role with other leading men, which is to not exist, or, failing that, to hide. The gut is antithetical to the leading man, insofar as girth signifies evil or mirth in the book of Hollywood semiotics. The gut is in the way, yet the history of Hollywood is littered with bottles establishing the gut in defiance of fan demand and box office viability. John Wayne, for example: the gut comes early and only gets worse with age. And so Hollywood resorts to magic, to cutaway shots and extra-terrestrial tailoring, to keep the gut at bay.

Brando's gut, we should note, is equally if not more a product of food as drink, vehicle of an astonishing appetite, as if his artistic intensity required vast amounts of fuel to maintain itself, or needed more than drink to drown its sorrows. Exactly when the gut emerges is debatable—does it creep in *On the Waterfront* (1954) under that shepherd's plaid lumberjack?—but it's unmistakably entrenched by *Sayonara* (1957), lurking beneath his carefully constructed kimono. The snakeskin jacket of *The Fugitive Kind* (1959) is a positive godsend to producers anxious to conceal his burgeoning pregnancy. The stress of directing and starring in *One Eyed Jacks* (1961) doubtless contributes to an increasing bulk restrained by *Star Trek*-like Western apparel, itself subject to continual modifications as he eats his way through the film. There follows the legendary fifty-two pairs of pants he split filming *Mutiny on the Bounty* (1962), the double necessary for certain far shots in *The Appaloosa* (1966) after Brando ate lunch. But it is between these two films that the gut makes its dramatic debut, albeit in the minor role of Sheriff Calder's gut in *The Chase* (1966), lending admirable realism to Brando's portrayal of a police officer in a small Southern town; this guy would have a gut, built of BBQ and beer. In Chaplin's *A Countess from Hong Kong* (1967)—a brilliant film few understand—the gut stretches out in its performance as diplomat Ogden Mears's gut, playing for comedy, for once, during the slapstick scenes, the way a gut's supposed to. This man too would have a gut, a gourmand's gut of embassy dinners, big steaks and mountains of baked potatoes. The gut here is in fine fettle.

By the time of John Huston's *Reflections in a Golden Eye* (1967), Brando's gut has become something of a ham, threatening to disrupt proceedings, woefully miscast as Major Weldon Penderton's gut. Cadet-instructing Major Penderton shouldn't have a gut; he should be firm, rigorous, but the producers couldn't get Brando unless they took the gut as well. Prodigious efforts are made to contain it through wardrobe, and their success might be gauged by home-movie footage of Brando on the set with Huston and Elizabeth Taylor, conferring before a horse-riding sequence. In amateur hands, the camera easily finds its way into Brando's tweed riding costume, disclosing a solid paunch Huston is at pains to minimize, no doubt wishing he was shooting slender original lead Montgomery Clift, who had to go and die on him. Just as the gut threatens to take over, however, Brando makes one last effort to part with his rival, slimming down for an attempted comeback in the cheapo New Wave–style thriller *The Night of the Following Day* (1968). The gut is conspicuous here by absence. It dictates the very tenor of the publicity, the trailer voiceover announcing "Brando—the *lean* hero you remember." It even shapes Brando's character, Bud the Chauffeur, who wears tight black clothes and continually tucks in his t-shirt to remind the audience of his leanness, to assure everyone the gut is really gone. The film was a failure, one of a string of failures brought on by Brando's desire to play unpleasant or evil characters, like *The Ugly American* (1963), as a way to inject political commentary into his work. Too, the film's failure indicates the irrelevance of the belly to Brando's appeal, a fact he clearly gambles on as he lets himself go.

The temporary exile of the gut is Brando's last concession to the popular will; rather than pander to it, he digs in deeper, starring in Pontecorvo's *Burn!* (1969), an astonishing exposé of the mechanism of colonialism. The gut's already back, slightly chastened, lending weight to Brando's portrayal of British agent provocateur Sir William Walker, particularly in his broken, brawling interim between his two missions to the Portuguese Antilles. Providing heft beneath his blouse, the gut allows Walker to plausibly brawl, disclosing a new aspect of the cerebral manipulator. He's not merely words, though they are his main weapon. In *The Godfather*, the gut is discreet, a subtle sign of Don Vito's age and success. Allowing Brando his Hollywood comeback, the gut instead looks to Europe for what is surely its definitive artistic turn, an understated yet virtuoso performance as Paul's gut in Bertolucci's *Last Tango in Paris* (1972). The gut shapes

Paul to no small degree, symbolizing, along with the introductory glimpse of baldspot, his state of ruin in the wake of his wife's suicide. His paunch expresses his character's forty-five years, the twenty-odd years of age difference between the lovers, accentuating the grotesqueness of the rape scene. The gut has relinquished its scene-stealing impulses and works in tandem with Brando for a fully integrated performance. Yet its restraint pays off, and the gut delivers a sterling performance in two scenes. The first occurs within Paul's hotel, where his wife's lover also lives. In what is surely one of the oddest details of his wife's absent presence, Paul and her lover meet dressed in identical plaid bathrobes, both purchased by the wife. Within the sequence, Brando owns up to his difficulty keeping off a gut, whereupon the lover shows Brando his secret to keeping a flat stomach: chin-ups! Somehow we know Paul won't even try, yet the moment is a definitive bonding scene in a world torn apart by inexplicable events. The second scene is, of course, the death scene in which Paul is shot in the gut by the woman whose love he has destroyed. As we watch Brando's face run through pain, shock, sorrow, and, most eerily, joy, the gut is off-camera, but its presence is unmistakable, as the lifeblood of Paul spills onto the balcony. Brando's face, in other words, is a sign of the gut's experience of the throes of death, and the closeness with which they execute this scene together signals a rapprochement between the belly and its bearer.

By *Apocalypse Now* (1979), Brando has given up; director Coppola desperately wants a lean, towering Colonel Walter Kurtz, but Brando has neglected to lose the promised weight. The weight is inconsistent with the character of Kurtz, who threw away the career path to generalship in order to train as a Green Beret to fight in Vietnam. Coppola hits on the device of cloaking Brando in shadow, which is effective filmmaking to be sure, but even the distraction of the actor's totally bald head is insufficient to conceal his girth. Kurtz is unambiguously bulky, yet Coppola needn't have worried. The gut here symbolizes Kurtz's fall into ruin, much like the decaying temple he inhabits. Like Brando, Kurtz has lost his discipline; the commando's gut is there to testify to his corruption through absolute power. By the time of *Don Juan DeMarco* (1995), Brando has ballooned to way over 300 pounds, the gut disappearing, finally, into a huge sea of fatness. The denim jacket Dr. Jack Mickler arrives in is a mythical coat; they simply don't make them cut to Brando's peculiar proportions. In this first scene, Brando is so infirm with weight, he has to be lifted on a crane in order to meet titular costar Johnny Depp. Brando's regard for Depp makes him a sort of successor, the only possible one in today's Hollywood, and their first scene together—in which they speak to each other in flawlessly maintained accents—is comic yet moving. It is clear Brando loses weight simply by having to act and he is somewhat "leaner" as the film goes on. Yet he is still breathless walking down a corridor, even getting out of a car. He has to be on his back for his love scene with Faye Dunaway, shot so close he is virtually just a head rolling back and forth to signify passion and arousal. Sadly the gut is on the sidelines, invisible, unable to work under these conditions. Yet by his last film, *The Score* (2001), in which he plays incorrigible fence Max, Brando has deflated considerably, "slimming" down to combat the effects of old age and declining health. The gut exists, here and there, a deflated bag unable to regain its former glory even though Brando steals each of his all-too-few scenes. It's a fine final turn in a so-so film for someone who'd stopped giving a shit long ago.

Yet even in ruin, in bad films made just for money, Brando thrills. In *The Formula* (1980), a real stinker starring a wreck of a George C. Scott, Brando's performance as the allegorically named oil executive Adam Steiffel utterly justifies the movie's existence, and it's characteristic of him to take on such an evil, anticapitalist role. Looking like Dick Cheney, Brando delivers a brilliant final scene. Drunk as a lord, momentarily forgetting his character's last name during a phone call, he delivers a searing indictment of the machinations of the oil industry, its manipulation of peoples and economies in the name of profit. In the midst of his attempts to persuade Scott of the reasonableness of this behavior, he opens a silver candy dish and offers his opponent a Milk Dud. "They're good," he says, with disconcerting solemnity. While Scott is on the phone thinking he's saving the world, Brando stands in the background, looking through the window in an unerring imitation of someone looking out a window, showing you something you hadn't quite noticed in human behavior. He sets a grandfather clock to his own watch, symbolizing the industry's control of the larger world, making it impossible to concentrate on Scott's corny dialogue. After the latter exits, Brando takes a final solo scene, making a phone call to a Swiss government official to undo Scott's delusory victory, purposely halting, in the name of oil, the development of new fuel technology. Throughout the film the gut takes on a supporting role, yet it is allowed one featured turn, in the first scene with

Adam Steiffel. At this point in his career, Scott has an enormous potbelly, one artfully concealed beneath another jean jacket that, at least, is more plausible than Brando's denim tent in *Don Juan DeMarco*. The only problem is Scott's head looks a mile behind his body. Clad in a Hollywood-tailored suit designed to conceal his gut, Brando walks up to meet Scott. Just as they shake hands, however, Brando tosses the coat open like a cape, upon which his gut flops out onscreen. Arrogantly thrown into view by Brando, the gut is at once a symbol of Steiffel's self-satisfaction, heedless of his personal appearance in favor of his appetites, and a hilarious actorly attempt to unnerve Scott, desperately sucking in. At the beginning of its filmic decline, the gut nonetheless contributes one of the best moments in the picture—clearly Brando shares some of Steiffel's arrogance—and it is here we might end, achronologically, in tribute to its classic performances, seemingly beyond the powers of most leading men today.

SELF-PORTRAIT AS DAVID LETTERMAN

When I host my eponymous talk show, I will feature segments on cave painting and automatic drawing at least once a month. The show will include a religious component, though I will heal not people but animals as the original faith veterinarian. I will draw my writers from the poetry scene for pithy skits on the latest theoretical trends. My bandleader will be Shock-G, and every now and then the show will be just him doing whatever he wants. Richard O. Moore will executive-produce and serve as announcer, and I'll use his connects to book impossible guests like James Baldwin, Duke Ellington, Frank O'Hara. The set will be a form of analytic cubism but the moving desk will introduce futurist principles. I'll incorporate my turtle Buster into my monologues like George Gobel riffing on Alice. Soon Buster will appear on my desk as my sidekick, making wisecracks in thought balloons. This part will backfire as he becomes too popular and I restrict his appearances, and the ensuing backlash kills our ratings. The show will be canceled in the sixth season due to controversial remarks on U.S. policy in the Middle East. Still it'll have been worth the ride, and people will marvel it lasted as long as it did. The time we have John Ashbery read the whole text of *Flow Chart*. The time Michael Palin reenacts Samuel Beckett's *Film*. The running gags with Clu Gulager. Ron Padgett vs. Google Translate. The Henri Michaux Ouija board incident, which leaves the Eastern Seaboard without electricity for nearly a weekend. DVDs will be impossible due to copyright issues, and most of the surviving footage will be from iPhones aimed at plasma screens. Each episode will begin with a Beyoncé thinkpiece and end with an impassioned plea to get your pets spayed or neutered. We won't be above a showcase showdown, but our thoughts will be more along the lines of *TV IQ Theme*. Pulling rabbits out of a hat or muscles from a shell. #knighthood4ringo.

PAUL BOWLES IN EL CERRITO

the marimbas and the marijuana were the only good things in the town. the men were violent and dirty. the women were made of stone. a tortilla might run up and smack your face. the doilies were straight unforgivable. there was a cactus the size of the grand coulee dam and a pencil the size of a lizard. a burro made of churros and a piñata stuffed with opinions. compared to my life as a mountain dweller, even the bums were city slickers. the wind always blew hard and cold. the marijuana and arhoolie records were the only good things in the town. there were ill-mannered goats as big as great danes, while the great danes themselves were like runty chihuahuas. the university presses were nothing to speak of and the abandoned monasteries less than picturesque. the palm trees were clenched like fists. the guitars were out of tune and the pianos had eighty-six keys. it was illegal for men to breastfeed in public. the ample parking and the marijuana were the only good things in the town. the flowers gave off the most foul odor. the sex offenders barely registered. there were no gas stations and it was a pain in the ass to go to the dentist. the internet was a broken wheel propped against a well, the telephone a buzzard on a shed. there were neon signs like giant banana leaves and stick bugs like you wouldn't believe. the gorge that lay below the town yawned and belched a puff of smoke, because the marijuana and the barbecue were the only good things in the town.

FOR ANDREW AND ROSE

SELF-PORTRAIT AS JAMES BOND

I'm feeling Italian and musical, so I'll take on the world that way: Biretta, claret, expense account. It's such a perfect place to start. In the next room or this very one, I dropped my Rolex and it exploded. That's me, that's my life. I'm not the only spy out here. What does it matter to you if I poison the odd prime minister? They'll make more. Another man as he stands right behind me looking in the mirror feels my presence in the crowd. I'm going to close my body now before he strikes like thunderball. I've seen diamonds cut through harder men. Hold one up and then caress it, then return it to the glove compartment of my hydroponic Lotus. There's some kind of magic inside me issued by Q Branch, but you'll never have my heart as it technically belongs to Her Majesty's government. That fatal kiss is all you need. I've seen places, faces, and smiled for a moment; you've seen my smile in a thousand dreams. The wild, abandoned side of me has left his gold paint in Miami, but my lies can't disguise what you fear. Love is a stranger who beckons you on. In the blink of an eye, I'll be there, too. With the cares of the world behind us, I'll file my report in the morning. Hey, driver, where we going?

FOR MATT CAPLES

ZEN OF NEZ

my pedal steel
spins its wheels
and i've hung
up my nudie
suit. i coldcream
the makeup off
shave my skull
with a razor
ready for the
inquisition, the spike
right through my
tongue. in these
my more christlike
moments i recall
my purpose forcibly
time to turn
in my commemorative
cufflinks, my hairshirt
has no sleeves
i make my
bed in a
pile of leaves
relinquish my rooms
at the plaza
still wine drips

from my lips
like blood, like
a bug i
found in my
salad. i rise
to the challenge
like feeding time
at the tank
and thank the
staff as they
pull me out
of the oxygen
tent, back into
civilization. my berlin
period will never
end at the
rate things are
going tonight. i'm
like the love
child of joan
rivers and larry
rivers and maybe
sam rivers too
i'm blowing through
chicago soon, so
catch me running
down a dream
of the grand

ennui in the
pump room's dignified
crapper. this time
a stark elegance
will characterize my
actions when i
emerge from behind
the curtain. will
my reinvention as
an ascetic mystic
spoil my chances
at that last
golden country great
or am i
fated to roam
the cruiseship and
county fair venues
of faded intelligentsia
it takes a
lot out of
me to be
the one to
see the mortal
remains remain but
someone is to
blame for the
indiscretions hectoring me

TRACTATUS

night ripens
& the whole
sky hangs

from a single
yellow nail

venus below
a dish of moon

below that
san francisco

it's like that
morning walk
i took on a hit
of weak acid

when the city
disclosed its
character to me

after a long
opacity

except in reverse
there's less light
in the world
right now

the world is
less explicable

the world is less
than is the case
since your late
removal from it

the most ordinary
thing in the world
is death, i hear you
somewhere say

& for once i choose
not to believe

venus glows
like topaz as if
you were there

while i walk
to the store
for whiskey

to give you
a proper wake

FOR RICHARD O. MOORE

TEN TEN-LINE POEMS

FOR PHILIP LAMANTIA

my mental block
is hot with cops
clubbing my clubbing
persona. the walls
always never end
still thinking of you
and unable to turn
the corner where
we last left off
but: to be continued

scene: better days
desk by the window
a dresser a bed bottles
in the fridge and you
standing there forgetting
what you stood up to
show me. you show me
you. it's enough. there's
a million books in this
place!

exhaling impossibly
huge clouds of
smoke and
hearing your
voice curl
through it
you called
getting high
turning on
it was both

your eyes wander
from your photograph
while you wonder what
i'm up to. overseeing
old haunts. what
you've seen is gone
as you are. here am i
and the building is
not the same but it's
the same building

uncatalogued, unrecorded
what you knew swarmed
like hummingbird wings
always buzzing around
you, like a dozen flaming

hula hoops, *ten bright*
balls bat the air. where'd
they go? the laws of
gravity dictate looking
up in silence

your voice could
encompass a universe
your love envelop decay
your word encircle
your light enrapture
and your hand strike
the collective blow as
the one who sang
the world's agonized
blood: you

incommunicable
experience of
visionary genius
unable to
synthesize
your intuitive
intelligence in
prose because
you were its
synthesis

leading you
by the hand
in the dark
so you don't
trip and fall
on the bricks
like tending the
one phoenix egg
in love and
silent terror

every week you found
the wine; every week:
new wine. the manic
accumulations: notebooks
ashtrays changepurses
the accumulated pain
of being who you were
who were you? saint
in an iron maiden as a
refuge from madness

i don't remember who
i was before we met
and now that you're
gone where am i?
somewhere else

where there's no
one like you and
the me i used to
be is equally
dead

THE CANTOS, THEN TACOS

(DICTATION FROM BARBARA GUEST)

the gong flares

les paul is more
withdrawn

curtain! curtain!

bypass mohawk craze

open failed boutique

dark hardens
and harkens

harnessing

yon drunken orchard
yon pretty field

not in *my*
los angeles   not on my budget

dear bloodandguts

we mustn't eat
chicken and waffles

more than once
a week

if it's not
against
the law
what is

cracking jokes
in two

a darkness
underneath

lends even this
vapor weight

what became of
the millennium

they used to speak of

(nostalgia for

that apocalypse!)

o dangerous passage of time

o opium dream

the poem

becomes

los angeles

by means of

mental geometry

rigid grid

on fluid spine

the colossal

squid's giant

eye

wider than a dinnerplate!

warms its cornea

against

oily human tentacles

supreme knuckle sandwich

this science

spume covered

kelp mouthed

swaddled

pain

tell me, poet, what is pain?

pain is the blank page

surrounding the poem

outside it

predominant

o unsaid pain

pain grew up
on a farm

pain slept in a loft

in los angeles
drinking vodka

pain slept in a lot

pain slept on zoloft

hooray pain

pain shuts its eyes

impelling itself

through the world

pain even became
a connoisseur

cosmetic pain

pain makes itself
dainty for you

in the blood green eye
of the national turbine

floating events still occur

on the street
a three year old
girl

plucks a dandelion's
empty stem

and hands it to me

saying

this is a flower from yesterday

later at the lake
two ten year old
boys

one pegs a goose
with a woodchip

goose departs, furious

i hit it—hear the noise it made?

this too investigation
of nature

or

future passion

los angeles fauna
roll on the flora

j'adore ça!

let perception write itself

let perception right itself

reluctant *flâneur*

speak to me only   with your eyes

eat the cantos, then tacos

let the radio play

in the metal brain

of los angeles

let the guitar fret

the gong gong

the tambour do what it do

give ’em hell, shoenberg

we are not prejudiced

behold yon motherfuckers

exercise caution
presumptive nominee

this a flower from yesterday

an apostrophe to everything

CELTIC LOVE SONG FOR SUZANNE

i have been a fortune in food stamps glued to a column of fire
a stitch in the hem of a robe of the united invisible boys choir
the third line in a badass tread of a steel-belted radial tire
i haven't been her lover; i have been, not at all

i've been the missing page of a paperback by marcel schwob
a post earring parked in a celebrity's dubious lobe
a bowdlerized propertius line recently restored to loeb
i haven't been her lover; i have been, not at all

i've been the fountain pen of an antique nation's philosopher
the organizational principle of the secret cosmic sock drawer
a fleck of spit on the lips of kurtz as they utter *the horror*
i haven't been her lover; i have been naught

i've been a vinyl lp crackling below snow white's glass casket
the ecstasy of yogi bear espying an unguarded pic-a-nic basket
the answer to a question so thoroughly tasteless i ask it
i haven't been her lover; i have been, not

i've been a native californian's blueprint for better orange juice
a single strand of bullion thread in the slipknot of a hangman's noose
a metaphysical punching bag for the ladies ski-team from belarus
i haven't been her lover; i haven't been shit

i’ve been a squeaktoy chewed upon by a pack of anonymous pugs
a grove of trees that came to life to kill a bunch of roman thugs
a detail in a harebrained scheme foiled by some meddling kids on drugs
and i have been her lover; i have been all